GODS & GODDESSES

OF THE ANCIENT WORLD

Frigg

BY VIRGINIA LOH-HAGAN

Gods and goddesses were the main characters of myths. Myths are traditional stories from ancient cultures. Storytellers answered questions about the world by creating exciting explanations. People thought myths were true. Myths explained the unexplainable. They helped people make sense of human behavior and nature. Today, we use science to explain the world. But people still love myths. Myths may not be literally true. But they have meaning. They tell us something about our history and culture.

45th Parallel Press

Published in the United States of America by Cherry Lake Publishing
Ann Arbor, Michigan
www.cherrylakepublishing.com

Content Adviser: Alexandra Krasowski, Worcester Art Museum, Harvard University (Extension School)
Reading Adviser: Marla Conn MS, Ed., Literacy specialist, Read-Ability, Inc.
Book Design: Jen Wahi

Photo Credits: © Jozef Klopacka/Shutterstock.com, 5, 21; © Tntk/Shutterstock.com, 6; © Kachalkina Veronika/Shutterstock.com, 8; © Miriam Doerr Martin Frommherz/Shutterstock.com, 11; © Nina Mikryukova/Shutterstock.com, 13; Elmer Boyd Smith/Public Domain/Wikimedia Commons, 17; © James_Cora/Shutterstock.com, 19; © AMV_80/Shutterstock.com, 23; © VeronArt16/Shutterstock.com, 24; © OceanBlack/Shutterstock.com, 27; © Volodymyr Tverdokhlib/Shutterstock.com, 29; © Howard David Johnson, 2018, Cover, 1, 15; Various art elements throughout, Shutterstock.com

45th Parallel Press is an imprint of Cherry Lake Publishing.

Library of Congress Cataloging-in-Publication Data

Names: Loh-Hagan, Virginia, author.
Title: Frigg / by Virginia Loh-Hagan.
Description: Ann Arbor : Cherry Lake Publishing, 2018. | Series: Gods and goddesses of the ancient world | Includes bibliographical references and index.
Identifiers: LCCN 2018003337 | ISBN 9781534129474 (hardcover) | ISBN 9781534131170 (pdf) | ISBN 9781534132672 (pbk.) | ISBN 9781534134379 (hosted ebook)
Subjects: LCSH: Frigg (Norse deity)—Juvenile literature.
Classification: LCC BL870.F6 L64 2018 | DDC 293/.2114—dc23
LC record available at https://lccn.loc.gov/2018003337

Printed in the United States of America
Corporate Graphics

ABOUT THE AUTHOR:

Dr. Virginia Loh-Hagan is an author, university professor, former classroom teacher, and curriculum designer. Like Frigg, she enjoys weaving. She knits and crochets. She lives in San Diego with her very tall husband and very naughty dogs. To learn more about her, visit www.virginialoh.com.

TABLE OF CONTENTS

CHAPTER 1

THE SUPREME MOTHER

Who is Frigg? Who are her family members? What does she do? What does she look like?

Frigg was a **Norse** goddess. Norse means coming from the Norway area. She was the wife of Odin. Odin was the father of all gods. He created the world. He created the gods. He created humans.

Frigg and Odin had two sons. Their names were Baldur and Hod. They were **twins**. Twins are people born at the same time. Baldur was the god of light. Hod was the god of darkness. He was blind. Odin had many lovers. He had many children with these women. Frigg took care of the children. She loved her stepchildren. Her most famous stepchild was Thor. Thor was the god of thunder.

Frigg was a sky goddess.

Frigg was the most powerful woman in Asgard.

Frigg was the goddess of marriage. She was the goddess of motherhood. She was the goddess of wisdom and peace. She was the goddess of household duties. She was the goddess of weaving. She was the goddess of spinning.

She protected women. She protected children. She weaved the fates. She also helped Odin rule. She and Odin ruled over **Asgard**. Asgard was the universe's center. It was heaven.

Family Tree

Parent: Fjorgynn (earth)

Spouse: Odin (father of all gods)

Children: Baldur (god of love and light) and Hod (god of winter and darkness, often called Hodr)

Maidens: Fulla (goddess of abundance), Gna (messenger of Frigg), Lofn (goddess of permission), Syn (goddess of boundaries), Var (goddess of oaths), Snotra (goddess of courtesy), Gefion (goddess of agriculture), Saga (goddess of history), Sjofn (goddess of affection), Hlin (goddess of refuge), Vor (giantess, seeress of Frigg), Eir (goddess of healing)

It was where the Aesir gods lived. There were two tribes of Norse gods and goddesses. They were the Aesir and the Vanir. Odin lived in Valaskjalf. This was the name of his house. It means "shelf of the dead."

Odin's house had a tall tower. His throne was at the top. He sat there. He saw over all the worlds. He saw everything. Frigg was the only other god who was allowed to sit with him. She was second in command.

Odin went on adventures a lot. Frigg ruled when he was gone. She liked to stay at her own house. Her home was called Fensalir. This means "**marsh hall**." Marshes are wetlands. Halls are grand houses.

Frigg was beautiful. She was tall. She had a crown with bird feathers. She wore white robes. She had a golden belt. Keys hung from her belt. She was known as the "lady of the hall."

Many Norse housewives also wore keys on belts.

CHAPTER 2

GIRL POWER

What are Frigg's powers? How is Frigg a good ruler?

Many Norse women worshiped Frigg. Frigg was very popular. She was the model of a loyal wife. She was the model of a perfect mother. She was the model of a perfect partner. She supported Odin. But she also had her own power.

She had magic. She could see the future. She knew what would happen to people. But she didn't share what she knew. She was a **volva**. A volva was someone who practiced **seidr**. Seidr was ancient Norse magic. It was about **destiny**. Destiny is fate. A volva could change destiny by weaving.

Frigg kept spirits up. She made others feel good. She had a drinking horn. She brought it everywhere. Her drinking horn was a cow's horn. It was used as a cup. Frigg used the drinking horn to celebrate others. She **toasted** warriors going to war. She toasted warriors coming home. Toast means to honor others. Frigg did this to wish good fortune. She wished good luck.

Volva goddesses traveled to different towns. They traded magic for things.

All in the Family

Eir was one of Frigg's maidens. She was a minor goddess. Her name means "help" or "mercy." She was a healer. She had medical skills. She was a good surgeon. Surgeons operate on bodies. She fixed sicknesses. She stopped bleeding. She saved people from dying. She was like an emergency room doctor. She oversaw women in childbirth. She was good at healing battlefield wounds. She might have been a Valkyrie. Valkyries were dark angels of death. They flew over battlefields. They took the strong soldiers. They took them to the underworld. They may have been Odin's daughters. Eir didn't take the dead. Instead, she chose who lived. She brought the soldiers back to life. Eir carried a red purse. The purse was magical. It had herbs and charms. Eir only taught her skills to other women.

Frigg was like a referee. She broke up fights.

Frigg was a good ruler. People and gods went to her. They sought help. They wanted advice. They asked her to solve problems. As the goddess of peace, she brought order.

There's a story about Frigg's leadership. There were two groups about to go to war. They were the Vandals and the Winnilers. Odin favored the Vandals. Frigg favored the Winnilers. Frigg begged Odin to let the Winnilers win. Odin said he'd give victory to the group he saw from his window when he awoke. He knew the Vandals were close. The Winnilers were farther away.

Odin slept. Frigg moved Odin's bed. She made him face a different window. She brought Winniler women to Odin's window. The women wore men's clothes. They put their hair around their faces. They looked like they had long beards.

Odin woke up. He saw the long beards. He kept his promise. So, the Winnilers won. They became known as the Langobards. This means "long beards."

Frigg outsmarted Odin.

CHAPTER 3

A MOTHER'S LOVE

What happens to Baldur? How does Frigg try to protect her son?

Frigg's favorite son was Baldur. Everyone loved Baldur. Baldur had dreams of dying. He told Frigg. Frigg got worried. She made a list of everything that could harm Baldur. She went all around the world. She begged people not to hurt Baldur. She got them to promise to keep him safe.

But Frigg made a mistake. She didn't think mistletoe was a problem. She thought it wasn't important. It was too little to do harm. Frigg went back to Fensalir. She told Baldur he was safe. She hosted a party. The gods wanted to test

Baldur's protection. They threw things at Baldur. Things bounced off him. Baldur didn't get hurt.

Loki was a trickster god. He tricked Frigg. He changed into a woman. He asked Frigg questions. Frigg told him

The gods liked to play games.

Real World Connection

Over 400 women from Borneo, Malaysia, got a world record. They made the longest rug ever. The rug is over 3,701 feet (1,128 meters) long. It's 28 inches (71 centimeters) wide. The women are from the Orang Ulu tribe. They're from a local women's group called Peng Doh Belaga. They're skilled rattan mat weavers. Rattan is a type of plant. It has long, thin stems. It's used to make furniture. The women wove the rug by hand. They didn't use any machines. Women all over Malaysia made rug pieces. Then the pieces were gathered in one place. They were joined together. The women are featured in a movie. The movie is called *Mat Weaver's Tale*. The women's goal was to save their craft. They wanted to promote it to the younger generations. They worked hard. Their backs ached. They stayed up all night to weave.

Loki liked playing tricks.

about mistletoe. Loki used that information. He made a mistletoe dart.

Loki got Hod to throw the dart at Baldur. Baldur fell down. He died. Everyone was sad. Loki ran away.

Frigg asked Hermod for help. Hermod was her stepson. He was the messenger of the gods. Frigg told Hermod to go to the **underworld**. The underworld was where dead souls lived. It was also called hell. It was ruled by Hel.

Hermod begged for Baldur's life. He said Baldur was loved and missed. Hel wanted him to prove it. She made a deal. She'd release Baldur if all living things cried for him.

Frigg begged everyone to cry for Baldur. But Loki stepped in. He disguised himself as Thok. Thok was a female giant. She refused to cry. So, Baldur couldn't return to the land of the living. This upset Frigg. She cried a lot.

Frigg knew Baldur was going to die. But she didn't have the powers to stop fate.

Hel was Loki's daughter.

CHAPTER 4

SPINNING STARS

How is Frigg connected to weaving? What are Frigg's tools?

Frigg was a weaver. She had a special spinning wheel. Spinning wheels make yarn. Her spinning wheel was bright. It was Orion's belt. Orion's belt is a **constellation**. Constellations are patterns made by stars. Orion's belt used to be known as Friggerock. This means "Frigg's **spindle**." Spindles are rods. They wind yarn for spinning. Stars look like they're spinning around Orion's belt. This looked like Frigg's spinning wheel.

Frigg pulled yarn from the clouds. She made clothes for the gods. She spun golden threads. She spun the threads of fate. She was known as the weaver of the thread of life. But she was not stronger than fate. Nobody can change the fabric of life.

Frigg also made clouds. She made sunshine. She made rain. This meant she helped crops grow.

Frigg's symbols included the full moon and silver.

Freya also had a magical cloak.

Frigg had a magical **cloak**. Cloaks are like capes. Frigg's cloak was made of feathers. She became a bird when she wore it. She could fly. She could travel anywhere she wanted. She could travel to different worlds. She could travel quickly.

She had a **chariot**. Chariots are carts. They have two wheels. They're pulled by animals. Frigg's animals were **rams**. Rams are male sheep. They have horns. They ram things with their heads.

Cross-Cultural Connection

Zhi Nu was a Chinese goddess. She was the goddess of weaving. She was the goddess of spinning. She was the goddess of crafts. She was the daughter of the Jade Emperor. She used clouds as yarn. She made beautiful silk robes for her father. She made beautiful designs. Her designs formed the constellations. Zhi Nu visited Earth. She met a cowboy. He was the heavenly official of cowherds. They fell in love. Zhi Nu stopped weaving. Her father became upset. He sent them into the sky. He used the Milky Way to keep them apart. They formed constellations. Zhi Nu became the Vega star. Her husband became the Altair star. The weaver and cowboy met once a year. They met on the seventh day of the seventh month. A flock of birds made a bridge for them to cross. Their happy tears caused rain.

CHAPTER 5

HAIL TO THE SKY WOMEN!

What do Frigg's maidens do? Who are the maidens?

King Rerir prayed to Frigg. He wanted a child. Frigg decided to help him. She sent him one of her **maidens**. Maidens are young women. The maiden turned into a crow. She brought the king an apple of fertility. The king's wife ate the apple. She had a baby.

Frigg had at least 12 maidens who served her. Frigg's maidens were **minor** goddesses. Minor means having less importance. The maidens weren't as well-known as Frigg. But they had their own powers. They had important jobs to do.

The maidens lived at Fensalir. They helped Frigg manage her house. They helped Frigg rule.

Frigg had three favorite maidens. Fulla was the goddess of **abundance**. Abundance means having a lot. Fulla held Frigg's jewelry. She took care of her shoes. She also knew all of Frigg's secrets.

Hlin was the goddess of **refuge**. Refuge means a safe place. Frigg decided who or what to protect. Then Hlin provided the protection. She kept danger away. She kissed tears away.

Frigg's maidens could also be moons.

Gna sent messages for Frigg. She traveled everywhere. She moved quickly. She rode her horse. Her horse was named

Explained By Science

Frigg's house was on marshes. Marshes are wetlands. Water soaks the area. It covers the land. It's wet all year long. Marshes are found all around the world. They're important wildlife habitats. Habitats are homes. Marshes support life. They provide food. They provide shelter. Many types of plants and animals live there. But marshes are disappearing. They're harmed by pollution. Pollution includes poisons, smog, and trash. Marshes are harmed by people. People build houses on marshes. This means there's less land for the plants and animals. Less land means less food. Marshes are at risk. People need to protect marshes. Marshes help stop floods. They soak in and store water. They're like sponges. Marshes help improve water quality. They have plants that clean dirty water. Marshes keep soil in place. This stops land from eroding. Eroding means wearing away.

Fulla wore a golden hood.

Hofvarpnir. This means “hoof kicker.” Gna’s horse ran through air and water.

Don’t anger the goddesses. Frigg had great powers. And she knew how to use them.

DID YOU KNOW?

- Frigg and Freya are often confused. Sometimes, they're the same character. In some stories, Freya is said to be Odin's wife. But Frigg and Freya are different characters. Frigg was an Aesir goddess. Freya was a Vanir goddess. Aesir and Vanir were the two main tribes of gods.
- Friday may have been named for Frigg. (Or it could have been named for Freya.)
- Lady's bedstraw is a plant. It's also known as "Frigg's grass." It's used to calm mothers during childbirth.
- Some women can't have children. They pray to Frigg. They ask her for children.
- Frigg's name means the "beloved one." Beloved means dearly loved.
- Frigg's name has been spelled different ways. Some spellings are Frea, Fija, Friia, Frig, and Friggja.
- Frigg was also known as the "weeping goddess." She cried when Baldur died. Some stories say she couldn't stop crying. She represents mothers who lose their children.
- Frigg's crown has heron feathers. Herons are wading birds. They live close to water. They like wetlands. They have long legs. They have long bills. Bills are like beaks.
- In some stories, Jord was Frigg's mother. Jord was also Thor's mother. This means Thor was her stepson and her half brother.
- Odin went on a journey to find wisdom. He was gone for a long time. Some stories say Frigg thought he was dead. So, she married Odin's two brothers. But Odin returned. He took Frigg back.

CONSIDER THIS!

TAKE A POSITION! Frigg seemed to favor Baldur. Baldur was her favorite son. Do you think this was fair? Why or why not? Argue your point with reasons and evidence.

SAY WHAT? Read the 45th Parallel Book about Freya. Compare Freya and Frigg. Explain how they're the same. Explain how they're different.

THINK ABOUT IT! Frigg defines what it means to be a wife. She defines what it means to be a mother. Compare Frigg to today's women. What would you like to change about women's roles in society?

LEARN MORE

Crossley-Holland, Kevin, and Jeffrey Alan Love (illust.). *Norse Myths: Tales of Odin, Thor and Loki.* Somerville, MA: Candlewick Studio, 2017.

Green, Roger Lancelyn, Michelle Paver, and Alan Langford. *Myths of the Norsemen.* London: Puffin, 2015.

Napoli, Donna Jo, and Christina Balit (illust.). *Treasury of Norse Mythology: Stories of Intrigue, Trickery, Love, and Revenge.* Washington, DC: National Geographic, 2015.

GLOSSARY

abundance (uh-BUHN-duns) having a lot

Asgard (AHS-gahrd) center of the universe where the Aesir gods lived

chariot (CHAR-ee-uht) two-wheeled cart pulled by animals

cloak (KLOHK) cape or coat

constellation (kon-stuh-LAY-shuhn) patterns of stars in the sky

destiny (DES-tuh-nee) fate, events that will happen

hall (HAWL) grand house

maidens (MAY-duhnz) young women serving in the court of a royal person

marsh (MAHRSH) wetland areas

minor (MYE-nur) having less importance

Norse (NORS) coming from the Norway area

rams (RAMZ) male sheep

refuge (REF-yooj) a safe place

seidr (SAY-der) ancient Norse magic

spindle (SPIN-dul) rod that winds yarn for spinning

toasted (TOHST-ed) honored

twins (TWINZ) children born at the same time from the same mother

underworld (UHN-dur-wurld) the place where the souls of dead people go after they die

volva (VOL-vuh) a type of Norse goddess who practices ancient magic

INDEX